BEING A HUMAN

LIFE IS MUCH BETTER WHEN YOU ARE LIVING IN THE PRESENT MOMENT

RIYANSHI SEHRAWAT

Copyright © Riyanshi Sehrawat
All Rights Reserved.

I would like to specially thank my parents.

Dear parents, I love you both a lot and appreciate your

effort and love in bringing me up to be a better individual.

Contents

Daddy and Mommy's advice

Daddy and Mommy always tell me

To be humble and kind

Some will say you're blind

But be the best you can be

Don't follow the crowd

It can get really loud

and you need time

Many won't like you

But they will pretend to

Please be very observing

If you wanna be surviving

Roads of Life

Some roads are smooth

Some are rough

Some are easy

Some are tough

But continue to walk

Because it will lead

To a destination even more

Beautiful than a dream.

Fears

These fears that hold you back

These fears that cut your track

These fears that kill your relief

These fears that cause disbelief

These fears that make you doubt

These fears that make you shout

The voice these fears hold

The whispers they have cold

So shake them away

Leave them in vague

Just fly away

Let your soul lead its way

Throw all these fears way

One day they will soon decay

Pain

If we show our pains to others

This world is ready to mock at us

If we hide our pain within ourselves

This world is ready to give us more pain.

Past

There comes a time

when you leave it all behind

it's really not a crime

There are better things to find

But you have to let go

I can be hard I know

But you got to be strong

You just can't hold on

To something long gone

It;s not easy to do

But you will get through

Oh! God

God you told me to wait a little

I wasn't happy about it

I fought an unending battle

At times I just wanted to quit

But you who created me

Said my reason will soon arrive

I've found it hard to believe

But you oh! god who is all knowing

Nothing is hidden from your face

and even when wind is blowing

you showed me your amazing grace

my life would be nothing today

After my doubts, you chose to stay

and I wanna thank you for everything

Coz I finally know I am with you

Time?

Time

Has always been there

It was the beginning,

And it's going to be the end.

It is forever changing, never the same as it was before.

It was a minute here,

A century there.

It saw the creating of everything,

and it will see the destruction of all.

It is a universal entity.

We regret when we waste it,

We wish we had more when we run out.

Howerever, when we do have it. we don't use it wisely.

We waste it, believing that we'll have it forever.

We don't realize that it'kk everntually leave us,

continuing long after we're gone.

It is neither a friend,

Nor an enemy.

Life is not in our Control

Life is full of surprises and shocks,

while we are planning and deciding,

Our next move,

our course of action,

It moves in opposite direction,

without warning,

while we spend a lifetime,

thinking and planning

about our future,

with our loved ones.

It takes a step further beyond our thinking

everything about life is always uncertain

the only thing that is constant about it is

it is always moving,

so keep moving,

Keep smiling always

I'm Busy

I'm busy

but not in the way

most people accept.

I am busy calming my fear

and finding my courage.

I'm busy getting in touch with what is real.

I'm busy growing things

and connecting with the natural world.

I'm busy questioning my answers.

I'm busy being present in my life.

Temporary

The storm always passes.

It won't last forever.

The rain always stops and

gives way to good weather.

The brightest and warmest of days still to come.

Please wait for the Sun.

The sunshine will come.

The Lost Nomad

Out in the sahara dessert

A lost nomad riding his camel

Molles and miles of sand

A beautiful sunset prevailing the sunset scene

Behind a scenic mountain

Though a bit mysterious

He decides to ride past

without looking back

Lost in the Beach

I once entered a mysterious land

and there were crystals of talc which was sand

the wind was cool as the sea

then i discovered something new in the sea,

Lost in that worldof my fantasy

with a lot of ecstatsy

There were a lot of ships

Sailing in the sea to strengthen their partnership,

There were numerous beautiful shells

and that land had a beautiful smell

This scene made my day,

one fine morning of May.

The Road less traveled

Winding roads that keep on going,

Rugged beaten path never slowing

A wondering traveler that goes on forth,

Foraging for the righteous source.

Slowing to a delay,

Contemplating on which way.

Struck with a decision,

Pondering the precision,

One path splicing into two,

Which way is the righteous way through?

Studying on forward,

Weighing probability to both paths to travel toward

Struck with the two options,

Reluctant with caution.

The first path is rocky and rough

Rarely taken, upon sight the path looks tough

No signs posted of the final destination.

Hesitant and in complete abjection.

Where the path goes?

That is completely unknown.

The second path looks smooth and worn.

Signs are posted and destination is forewarn.

Peering on forward,

Obviously, this is the path most travel toward

But pondering on the road already traveled,

And dwelling on the compelling traveled distance.

Shall the traveler keep on and hold persistence?

Or decide to go with ease

Finally let the struggle seize.

Thinking when the traveler was young,

An instructor made a statement that stuck in the young one's
mind and hung,

The young traveler was told,

That their story unfolds,

Some of us young travelers will show,

Greatness and choose to be bold,

Some will be weak and easily fold,

The instructor continued and said;

The majority of souls are sheep,

Scared of being subjugation so slowly they

Wonder, remaining weak.

Slowly grazing,

Dumfounded minds stuck to mazing.

These souls are sheep because they except the defeat.

Sheep follow a leader and stay in retreat.

As for the rest of the very few souls,

They have greater paths to unfold,

These souls are herding dogs.

Leaders rugged and strong.

Not scared of which path is wrong

Fearless of the path unknown

Staring up ahead,

The traveler decides to go for the path hardly lead.

The traveler will not accept defeat,

Absolutely refuses to be sheep.

Will not follow the rest of the cattle,

The traveler shall go on the strong and lead the battle.

I will continue to lead less traveled.

I would like to thank you for reading my short book till it's end.
Last but not the least.

P utting words

O n a paper to

E xpress

T houghts for me

R ight to

Y our heart

I would like to take a favour from you all please if there is any
kind of mistake -
email- riyanshisehrawat80@gmail.com